A Civilization Project Book

AZTECS

BY SUSAN PURDY
AND CASS R. SANDAK

Illustrations and diagrams by Pamela Ford Johnson

Franklin Watts   New York/London/Toronto/Sydney   1982

Contents

A Remarkable Civilization   **3**

Glyphs and Codices   **6**

Day Signs and Numbers   **8**

Mosaic Sun God Mask   **11**

Foods from the New World   **14**

Shields for Battle   **16**

A Decorated Cloak   **18**

Carved Relief of Tenochtitlan   **21**

An Aztec Drum   **24**

Aztec Cocoa Jug   **27**

Eagle Knight Helmet   **29**

Index   **32**

Library of Congress Cataloging in Publication Data

Purdy, Susan Gold
  The Aztecs.

  (A Civilization project book)
  Includes index.
  Summary: Describes some of the achievements of
Aztec civilization and includes instructions for re-
producing Aztec masks, shields, cloaks, carvings,
drums, jugs, helmets, and foods.
   1. Aztecs—Juvenile literature. 2. Indian
craft—Juvenile literature. [1. Aztecs. 2. Indians
of Mexico. 3. Indian craft. 4. Handicraft.]
I. Sandak, Cass R. II. Title. III. Series.
F1219.73.P87   972'.01   82-4945
ISBN 0-531-04455-6   AACR2

A Remarkable Civilization

The Aztecs were Indian people who controlled an empire in central Mexico when the Spaniards opened up the New World to exploration, conquest, and settlement. Under Hernando Cortes, the Spanish reached Mexico in 1519, when the Aztec civilization was at its height.

The Aztecs came from the north and arrived in the so-called Valley of Mexico in the twelfth century. This area is located between mountain ranges in the middle of the country halfway between the Gulf of Mexico and the Pacific Ocean. The Aztecs were nomadic until they established their capital at Tenochtitlan.

Aztec civilization was not the true creation of the Aztecs. Their artistic and technical achievements were based on the more advanced cultures of the Toltecs, Mayans, and Zapotecs, earlier tribes they conquered and displaced. Aztec culture combined elements of these earlier civilizations. Their language is related to that of several of the Indian tribes of the southwestern United States.

Aztecs developed a culture that included a distinctive stone wheel calendar; their own methods of weaving cotton, feathers, and maguey fibers; sculpture in hard and soft stone; engineering for building and fortifications; jewelry making with jade, turquoise, and other semiprecious stones; metalwork in copper, silver, and gold; music; and picture writing.

Aztec society was based on families and clans. Clans had their own elected officials and representatives. Land was held in common by the clans. Citizens were protected from injustice by a strict legal code and court system that punished wrongdoers severely. A charge of theft or drunkenness might warrant the death penalty. The administration of justice was swift and severe.

The Aztecs were a warlike people. Military service was a means by which a warrior could raise his standing in society through bravery in battle.

The Aztec capital of Tenochtitlan was built on a huge lake. The Aztecs constructed islands in the lake using large basketlike frameworks that they filled with soil. On the islands they built gleaming palaces and huge stepped pyramids surmounted by splendid temples. Long aqueducts carried pure drinking water into the heart of the city from the mountains.

Most farmers lived in huts made of wattle and daub. Farmers raised crops of corn, beans, peppers, squash, avocados, cocoa, tomatoes, sweet potatoes, tobacco, and cotton. Turkeys and dogs were the only domesticated animals. Wealthier people had more permanent houses built of stone or mud bricks. These more elaborate structures were often built around a central courtyard.

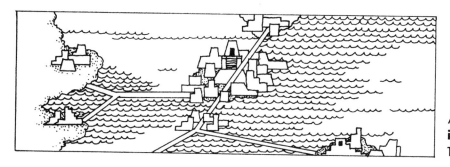

A view of the islands in the lake at Tenochtitlan

The Aztec religion affected every aspect of life. Powerful priests performed ritualistic human sacrifices. The victims were either captives taken in battle or citizens chosen by lot. Astronomy, the calendar, writing, and written records were all facets of religious life. Every hour of the day was under the power of different deities, and the gods were constantly appeased through elaborate ceremonies and rituals.

Despite the luxuries and achievements of their civilization, the Aztecs lacked the wheel, the axle, and pack animals. All heavy labor was done by humans. All trade was conducted by means of a barter system, since the Aztecs did not use money. Expensive items were often assigned a value in terms of cotton cloaks or copper spearheads. Cocoa beans were used as money for cheaper items.

The civilization collapsed with the coming of the Spanish. The Aztecs had established an unstable political empire by subjugating many of their neighboring Mexican tribes; in turn, many of these people helped the Spanish overthrow the Aztecs. The Spaniards killed the last of the Aztec emperors, Montezuma, and probably half the Aztec population. They leveled Tenochtitlan, and on its site founded Mexico City, now the world's largest city.

Even though the Aztec civilization disappeared, it left behind many products and foods that we still use. Rubber, vanilla, cocoa beans, tomatoes, and sweet potatoes are just some of them. Such modern English words as *tomato* and *ocelot* come directly from Nahuatl, the language of the Aztecs.

Many of the Indians who now live in the area of Mexico City are descended from the Aztecs. Sociologists say that there are about three thousand pure-blooded Aztec Indians living in the Valley of Mexico today who still speak the ancient Nahuatl language.

Glyphs and Codices

The Aztec language was called Nahuatl. The Aztecs used a form of picture writing, called hieroglyphics, to write down their laws and their stories of the past. A glyph showed an individual object or person; sometimes glyphs were combined to make up longer words. Simple glyphs were used for words like *tree*, *teeth*, and *stone*. The sign for traveling was a foot. Another sign stood for the emperor Montezuma (see examples). The name of the Aztec capital was the combination word Tenochtitlan, meaning cactus-stone. It was made up of the words for cactus, *noctli*, and stone, *tena*.

The Aztecs wrote in picture books called *codices*. A codex was made from long strips of paper or pounded fiber, folded like an accordion. The fiber came from the inner bark of the wild fig tree. The bark was stripped, soaked in lime water, pounded with stone, dried, and then coated with starch to make it smooth and white. Glyphs were painted on with animal, vegetable, or mineral dyes thickened with resin. Some codices had front and back covers made from animal hide, bark, or wooden strips. A few original Aztec codices can be seen in museums. Some were written before the Spanish Conquest, but others were written after the Indians learned Spanish. Codices are sometimes written in Aztec glyphs, sometimes in Spanish, or in a combination of both. They tell about Aztec history, speeches, songs, rituals, astronomy, and prophecy.

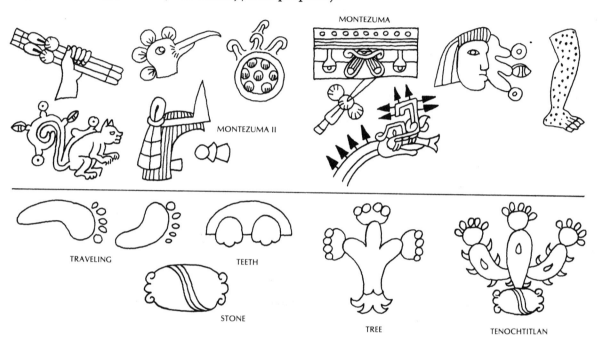

1. Make a codex from folded paper (See pages 9 and 10).

2. Use the Aztec glyphs shown here to tell a simple story in picture writing. Or make up your own symbols.

3. Write down your Aztec hieroglyphic story on a folded paper codex, as in Figure 1.

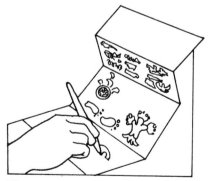

Figure 1

**An Aztec
calendar stone**

Day Signs and Numbers

The Aztecs used a number system based upon 20 for their calendars and for trade. Symbols represented the numbers dots or pictures of fingers represented 1 through 19; a flag meant 20; a single feather meant 400; a bag with tassels, 8,000.

The Aztecs had a remarkably sophisticated understanding of time. They had a calendar called the *tonalpohualli*, or "count of days." The Aztec year was divided into eighteen months of twenty days each. In addition, there were five "unlucky" or "hollow" days to complete the 365 days of the solar year. Children born on these unlucky days were given Aztec names such as "worthless." They lived under a cloud and felt fortune had betrayed them.

Materials you will need:

Strip of flexible white paper, 5 inches (12.5 cm) × 48 inches (120 cm); two pieces of leather, bark, or thin wood (as from a shingle), each 5 inches (12.5 cm) × 6 inches (15 cm); a thin reed; crushed berry or beet juice for ink; paints and brushes or felt-tipped pens; ruler; glue

1. Fold the strip of paper into 6-inch (15-cm) long panels using a fan or accordion fold as in Figure 1. There will be eight panels in all, each 5 inches (12.5 cm) wide and 6 inches (15 cm) long.

2. Glue the leather, wood, or bark covers onto the outside of the first and last panels, as in Figure 2. Press them flat until the glue dries.

3. Decorate the covers with Aztec signs and symbols or with the title of your codex: AZTEC DAY SIGNS AND NUMBERS.

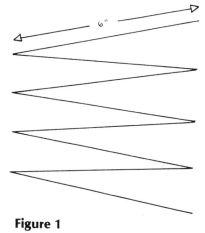

Figure 1

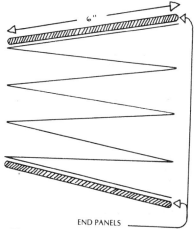

END PANELS

Figure 2

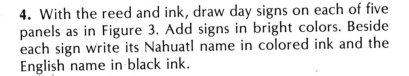

4. With the reed and ink, draw day signs on each of five panels as in Figure 3. Add signs in bright colors. Beside each sign write its Nahuatl name in colored ink and the English name in black ink.

5. On the sixth panel, draw the signs for the numbers from 1 to 10.

6. On the seventh panel draw the signs for 20, 80, 400, and 8,000.

7. On the last panel, show examples of counted items.

8. When the inks or paints are dry, refold your codex as shown in Figure 4.

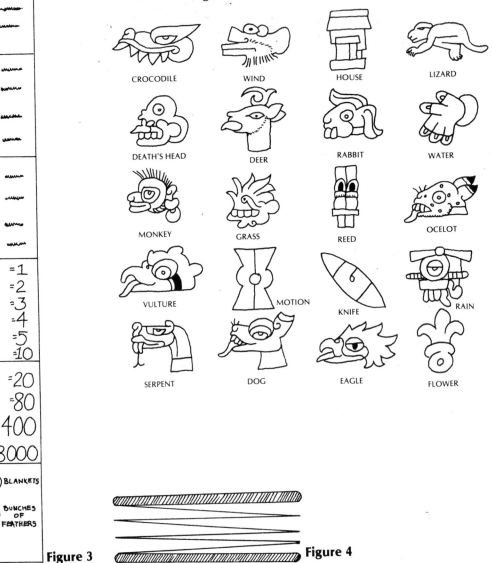

CROCODILE   WIND   HOUSE   LIZARD

DEATH'S HEAD   DEER   RABBIT   WATER

MONKEY   GRASS   REED   OCELOT

VULTURE   MOTION   KNIFE   RAIN

SERPENT   DOG   EAGLE   FLOWER

Figure 3

Figure 4

1

2

3

4

5

6

7

8

= 1
= 2
= 3
= 4
= 5
= 10
= 20
= 80
= 400
= 8000
= 400 BLANKETS
= 80 BUNCHES OF FEATHERS

Mosaic Sun God Mask

The Aztecs were a "people of the sun." Their entire religion was based upon the rising and setting of the sun. Aztec rituals were designed to perpetuate this cycle, since they believed that without their rituals, the cycle would stop and the world would end. They worshiped *Huitzilopochtli*, the god of war, who was also a sun god, and they worshiped *Tonatiuh*, another sun god. They believed the sun needed blood to have the strength to rise and that human hearts were the sun's favorite food. The ritual victims were often slaves or prisoners of war. They were costumed and well-treated, feasted, and then sacrificed on a temple altar. The victims were called the "children of the sun." It was considered an honor to be able to join the gods.

The Aztecs made mosaic masks, weapons, and ceremonial objects such as sacrificial knives. They used small bits of turquoise, jade, and shell to make their mosaics. The mask of the sun god Tonatiuh, on whom this model is based, is made of turquoise. The eyes and teeth are made of inlaid shell.

Materials you will need:

Salt dough, white glue, cotton-tipped swabs, paper towels, tweezers, eggshells, an empty clean white plastic bottle, scissors or knife, blue or black tempera paint, brush, food coloring or dye

1. Break eggshells into small pieces and dye them different shades of blue and blue-green by soaking them in food coloring or dye.

2. Spread the dyed eggshell bits out to dry on layers of paper towels.

3. Prepare salt dough (see box) and model a mask in the form of a human face, about 10 inches (25 cm) high. Build up a fairly realistic nose with nostrils, a wide, arched brow over the eyes, and deep-set eye sockets with horizontal oval eyes, as in Figure 1. The mouth should be a horizontal strip about ½ inch (1.25 cm) wide.

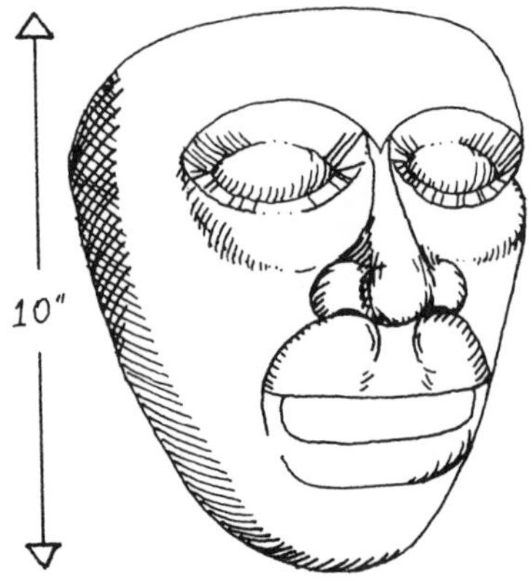

10"

Figure 1

SALT DOUGH RECIPE

1 cup salt
2 cups all-purpose flour
1 cup water
2-3 drops vegetable oil

Mix the ingredients together and roll out. Shape the dough. Sun-dry the pieces or bake them at 200°F (93°C) for about two hours for ¼-inch (.6-cm) thick pieces, longer for thicker pieces. Or bake at 200°F. (93°C) overnight with door of oven ajar. Do not use higher temperature or pieces will turn brown and crack. The purpose of baking is to dehydrate the dough, *not* to bake it. Dried pieces may be sanded before painting.

4. When the clay mask is thoroughly dry, paint it with a coat of black or blue paint.

5. Let the paint dry.

6. Glue on colored eggshell bits. To do this, dip a cotton swab into white glue, then dab the glue on the back of the piece of eggshell. Use tweezers to pick up the eggshell. Glue the bits in more or less even rows, outlining the arch of the eyebrows, down the center line of the nose, and around the edges of the mouth and lip area. Then glue the rest of the pieces in rows close together, so that you fill in all areas except the mouth, eyes, and a spot between the brows at the bridge of the nose (Figure 2).

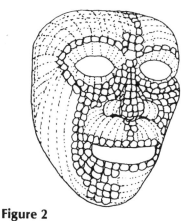

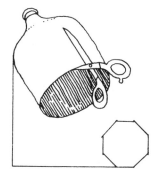

Figure 2

7. Cut a hexagonal piece of white plastic bottle about ½ inch (1.25 cm) across, as in Figure 3.

8. Glue this piece between the eyebrows (see Figure 4).

9. Cut two plastic oval eyes and seven teeth (Figure 4) and glue them in place.

10. Paint black or dark blue pupils in the centers of the eyes.

Figure 3

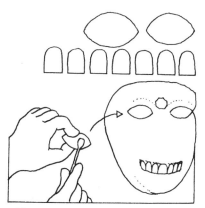

Figure 4

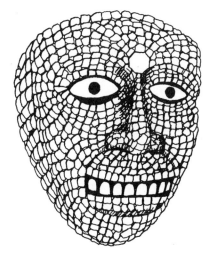

13

Foods from the New World

The Aztecs ate a variety of foods. Even the simplest diet consisted of maize in the form of maize cakes, porridge, and tamales. Beans, seeds, wild plants, and insects such as agave worms and ants were also eaten. Foods were usually highly spiced; amaranth, sage, and peppers were used for seasoning. There was no early morning breakfast, but after some work, a bowl of maize porridge, either sweetened with honey or seasoned with pimento, was served. Rich men and dignitaries drank cocoa, sweetened or spiced. The main meal was at midday, the hottest hour of the day. Commoners drank water and ate maize cakes, beans, pimento or tomato sauce, and sometimes tamales. Meat was rarely served. The Aztecs had neither fat nor oil; everything was either grilled or boiled.

The Aztecs had no cattle. Their meat came solely from game—pheasants, partridges, doves, crows, pigeons, ducks, deer, boars, hares, rabbits—and their two domesticated animals, turkeys and dogs. They also enjoyed many water creatures: frogs, tadpoles, shrimp, waterflies, and waterfly eggs, which they served as a sort of caviar. They had a wide variety of vegetables native to their area, including sweet and white potatoes, tomatoes, and pimentos. These vegetables were unique to the New World. Sixteenth-century Spanish explorers introduced them, along with chocolate, to the rest of the world.

FIRE-BAKED SWEET POTATO

Ingredients:
Whole sweet potatoes
Aluminum foil
Tomatoes
Pimentos

1. Scrub the sweet potatoes and wrap them in foil. Stick them among the coals of a fire.

2. Bake about an hour, or until the potato can be pierced easily with the tines of a fork.

3. Unwrap the foil and cut the potatoes open.

4. Serve mashed or sliced, with fresh sliced tomatoes alongside and topped with fresh pimentos.

AZTEC HOT COCOA

Ingredients: (for 3 servings, 1 cup each)
1½ squares unsweetened Baker's chocolate (*or a*
    2-ounce [56-g] cake of Mexican chocolate bought in
    a specialty food shop)
3 tablespoons honey
Pinch of salt
1 cup water
½ teaspoon vanilla extract
2 cups milk
Optional: ½ teaspoon cinnamon plus ¼ teaspoon
    nutmeg

1. Combine the chocolate, honey, salt, and water in double boiler over medium heat.

2. Stir with a wooden spoon until the chocolate is melted and the mixture is creamy and smooth.

3. Add milk and vanilla, stirring well, and heat until warm enough to drink.

4. Beat the mixture with an eggbeater until foamy.

5. For a modern Mexican variation, add cinnamon and nutmeg (or even ¼ teaspoon of instant coffee) to the other ingredients.

Shields for Battle

Aztec warriors used round shields made of wood or reeds. These shields were decorated with feathers, mosaics, or metal ornaments. A shield like this was called a *chimalli*. It was used with a wooden sword, the *macuahiutl*. The macuahuitl had a sharp cutting edge made of obsidian, a hard, black, shiny volcanic rock. Shields were used in battle and were given as gifts to conquering tribes. They were also used as a unit of trade. Shields bore a wide variety of motifs. Some designs were decorative, while others symbolized the rank or exploits of the bearer. Shields were painted bright red, white, yellow-gold, blue, green, or black.

Materials you will need:
Lid from a plastic or metal garbage can (or other round container), or an 18-inch (45-cm) circle of stiff cardboard; tape or glue; old leather belt or stiff paper; stapler; scissors or knife; eight or more long feathers; tempera paint and brushes, pencil, colored paper, felt, or fabric

1. Prepare your basic disc. A plastic or metal lid will usually have a handle. If you use a flat disc without a handle, make one as shown in Figure 1.
a. Make two slits in the center of the disk 6 inches (15 cm) apart.
b. Insert the ends of an old leather belt or a piece of stiff paper folded into a strap about 14 to 16 inches (35 to 40 cm) long.
c. Staple, tack, or glue the ends of the strap onto the back side of the shield.

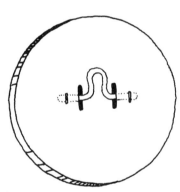

Figure 1

Figure 2

2. Measure and cut out a solid piece of colored paper, felt, or fabric the same size as your shield. On this, sketch your design. You can use the motifs shown in Figure 2.

3. Paint your design, or use overlapping rows of colored feathers, filling in one area at a time. Work from the bottom up. In the top row, glue one row of feathers sideways over the stems (see Figure 3).

4. When you have finished the design, glue it onto the front of your shield.

5. Turn the shield over, back side up. Tape or glue a row of at least eight very long, colorful feathers along the bottom edge as shown in Figure 4. Their stems should be at the bottom of the shield. Their tips should hang down below the shield as far as possible. Use a piece of tape to cover the stems neatly.

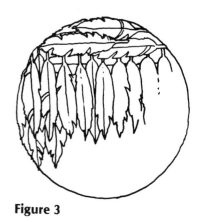

Figure 3

Figure 4

A Decorated Cloak

The basic article of Aztec clothing was the cloak. A cloak, or *tilmatli*, was worn by both men and women.

Cloaks for ordinary people were woven of agave fiber. People of higher rank used cotton. The higher the rank, the more elaborately decorated the cloak was. Cloaks were made in a variety of rich and colorful patterns. For protection from the cold, rabbit hair was threaded through the cloth or it was reinforced with feathers. Colored or dyed feathers were also used for purely decorative cloaks. The tilmatli were worn knotted on one shoulder.

The emperor was the only one allowed to wear the royal color: the blue-green color of turquoise stone. This was known as the *xiuhtilmatli*, "the turquoise cloak."

Cloak design for nobility

Cloaks were so important that a marriage ceremony was performed by having husband and wife literally "tie the knot" by joining their cloaks together at one corner.

Weaving was done by women. Certain provinces were famous for their splendid colored embroideries and weavings, and these paid heavy tribute (taxes) in woven goods—cloaks, loincloths, and skirts. The brightly colored patterns included stylized motifs such as suns, shells, jewels, fish, cacti, feathers, butterflies, skins of tigers, snakes, or rabbits, and abstract geometric shapes. Priests wore tilmatli decorated with skulls and bones.

Materials you will need:
A piece of soft cotton or light wool about 42 inches (106 cm) × 30 inches (76 cm), in white or a light color; scrap paper; fabric paint and brushes, or permanent felt-tipped markers; pencil; chalk; scissors; ruler; needle and thread; straight pins; colored feathers (optional)

1. Iron the fabric flat.

2. Roll over, pin, iron, and stitch a hem ½ inch (1.25 cm) wide around all edges of the fabric, as in Figure 1.

3. Remove the pins.

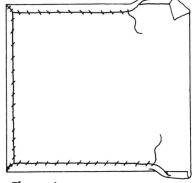

Figure 1

Cloak design for lesser-ranked people

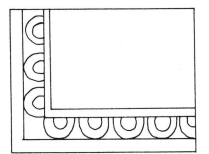

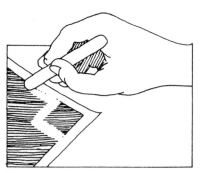

4. Use a pencil or chalk to plan your design on scrap paper, as in Figure 2.

5. Copy the design with chalk or light pencil onto the fabric, as in Figure 3.

6. Paint the design with fabric paint (follow the manufacturer's instructions).

Figure 2

7. If you like, you can fill in some areas of the design by sewing on dyed or colored feathers. You may want to make a border of feathers all around the edges; or just sew a few in a pattern or at random. To use the feathers, begin working on the bottom edge of the fabric, stitching the feather stems to the cloth. Add overlapping rows, as in Figure 4, stitching them down until you reach the top row. To cover the sharp quill ends, sew or glue on one row sideways over the ends, or sew an edge of colored fabric over the ends of the quills.

Figure 3

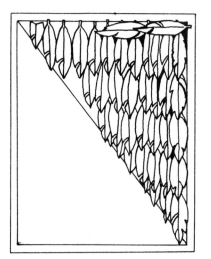

Figure 4

Carved Relief of Tenochtitlan

Aztec artisans were famous for the magnificent stone bas-reliefs they carved on their temple walls. Nearly every surface of temple statues or ritual objects was richly ornamented. This was done most often to express Aztec cultural beliefs and religious symbolism.

According to Aztec legend, *Tenochtitlan*, the name of the Aztec capital, means "place of the cactus." It was believed that long ago the Aztec people were wandering in search of a land in which to live. They saw a great eagle perched on a cactus growing out of a large rock among the reeds of a lagoon. The eagle was devouring a snake. On this site, the Aztecs founded their capital Tenochtitlan. The portrayal of this scene, the eagle on the cactus on the rock, is used symbolically to evoke the origin of the city. The eagle is the symbol of the great god, Huitzilopochtli, god of sun and war. With this emblem the Aztecs reminded themselves that even at the height of their glory they should not forget that their city had been founded in a swamp by a homeless tribe.

Our model is a relief carving in clay, illustrating the origin of the name of the Aztec capital.

Figure 1

Figure 2

Materials you will need:
Self-hardening clay or salt dough (see page 12), rolling pin, ruler, cardboard for base, modeling tools, toothpick or pencil, scrap paper, tempera paints and brushes, sandpaper, spray shellac

1. Prepare clay or dough and roll it out into a slab about 1 inch (2.5 cm) thick and 12 inches (30 cm) square.

2. With a pencil, sketch the design shown in Figure 1 onto scrap paper that is 12 inches (30 cm) square. Make the rectangular outer border first, with a diagonal cross within it. Then, over the center of the cross, draw a circle. In the circle draw the stylized glyph form of the rock topped by the three-branched cactus. On top of this sits the eagle (Figure 2).

3. Place your sketch right side up on top of the rolled-out clay. Line up the paper edges with the slab edges.

4. Draw over your lines with a sharp pencil or toothpick, as in Figure 3. (This will transfer the design onto the clay.) Lift the paper.

5. Use a straight cutting tool, like the tip of a knife, to outline the border and the cross lines, cutting down about ⅛ inch (.3 cm) into the slab.

FEATHER DETAIL

Figure 3

22

6. Remove the flat areas between the edged lines by scooping out the spaces that are shaded areas in Figure 1. Work these areas until they are flat and smooth—with the border lines and cross raised—and have straight, neat edges, as in Figure 4.

7. Paint the decorative emblem or carve it out in bas-relief within the circle. To make your carving, leave a narrow border around the circle. Then remove the background between the border ring and the eagle, cactus, and rock figures. The figures will be raised in relief. (See Figure 5.) Sculpt details like feathers and cactus needles by adding bits of clay or scratching out lines where needed.

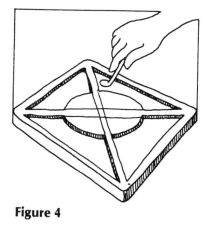

Figure 4

8. Let the clay dry thoroughly overnight.

9. Sand the rough edges of the slab.

10. Paint the design with bright colors. Paint geometric patterns along the border strips and crossed lines, as in Figure 6.

11. For gloss and permanence, coat your clay emblem with shellac or spray urethane.

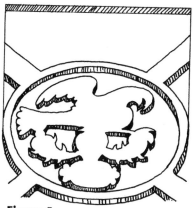

Figure 5

Figure 6

An Aztec Drum

The Aztecs loved singing and dancing, music, poetry, and oratory. At feasts, banquets, and ceremonies, costumed men and women danced to music. Dancing was a way of serving the gods and calling on their favor by using one's whole body.

We know almost nothing about Aztec music, since it was not written down. We know that it was rhythmic, but we do not know what it sounded like. The music seems not to have been important in itself, but it helped the singers and dancers keep time.

Percussion instruments were the most important. The upright drum was called the *huehuetl* and the two-toned wooden drum was the *teponaztli*. The drums were made of clay and wood, with snakeskins or animal hides stretched over the top and tied around the rim with cord. Other noisemakers included notched bones which were scraped with a stick and a variety of rattles.

Our model is a *huehuetl*, or upright single-headed drum, decorated with traditional motifs.

Materials you will need:
Large tin can, or any large cylindrical form, preferably of wood, metal, or heavy plastic; crayon, paints and brushes, or permanent felt-tipped pens; string or heavy-duty rubber bands; heavy plastic sheeting or discarded rubber inner tube; scissors; colored paper (a piece long enough to wrap around the drum like a skirt)

1. Empty and clean the can. The bigger the can is, the deeper the tone will be; the smaller the can, the higher the tone.

2. Remove one or both ends of the cylinder, as in Figure 1. If the bottom of the drum is open, the resonance will be greater and the sound will be louder.

3. If you wish, paint the outer surface a solid color and let the paint dry.

4. Set one end of the drum over the plastic or inner tube and draw around the rim, as in Figure 2.

5. Draw another circle about 3 inches (7.5 cm) wider than the rim of the cylinder (Figure 3) all around the outside of the rim outline.

6. Cut around the larger outer circle.

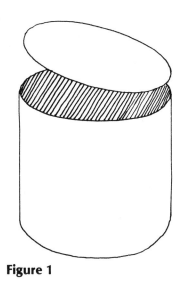

Figure 1

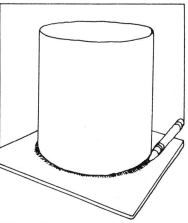

Figure 2

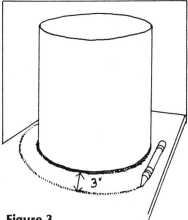

Figure 3

Suggested drum motifs

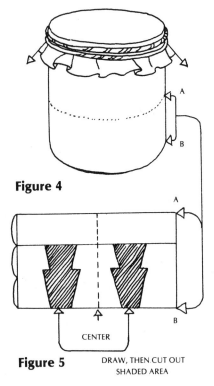

Figure 4

Figure 5 DRAW, THEN CUT OUT
SHADED AREA

CENTER

7. Stretch this circle of rubber or plastic over the top of the cylinder.

8. Secure the drum top at the rim with several *very* tight wraps of string or several tight-fitting, heavy-duty rubber bands, as in Figure 4.

9. Pull the edge of the drum top down over the cylinder. Pull on opposite sides at once, to make the skin taut and to remove any wrinkles, as in Figure 4.

10. The drum may be decorated on the sides by painting the motifs shown at the top of the page, or by gluing on a paper "skirt," cut in the zig-zag pattern shown in Figure 5. Figure 6 shows the finished drum.

11. The drum is now ready to be played. You can use your hand, a pencil, or a stick.

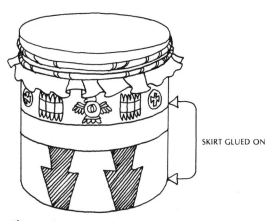

SKIRT GLUED ON

Figure 6

Aztec Cocoa Jug

The cocoa bean was an important element in Aztec life. Traders used the beans for money and they were used to pay taxes. Rich people and dignitaries and their families enjoyed *xocoatl*, a drink made from the bean. Vendors sold xocoatl on the streets. The Aztecs drank their cocoa flavored. It was either sweetened with vanilla-scented honey, or mixed with green maize, *octli*, (fermented agave sap), or pimento.

The word *xocoatl*, or chocolate, has been adopted into most European languages. The cocoa bean and the chocolate made from it came to us from the Aztecs.

Our model is of a clay cocoa jug, the type typically used in an Aztec household to hold the beverage.

Materials you will need
Self-hardening clay, tempera paints and brushes, paper, scissors, pencil, modeling tools, water in can, ruler or tape measure

1. Roll the clay into coils and build up a round jug base. Make the form as even as you can, as in Figure 1.

2. Smooth the coils as you build them up, making a smooth surface on the outside. Use a little water to dampen the clay so that the coils adhere to each other.

3. Make a paper pattern for the neck and spout, as in Figure 2. The base line A-B must be wide enough to reach around and overlap at the top opening of the jug. Measure this opening and make your paper pattern to fit it, as in Figure 2. Fold the pattern in half to cut an even shape.

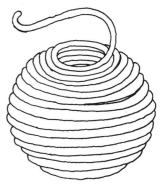

Figure 1

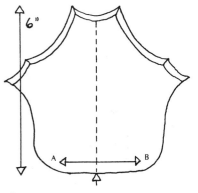

6"

Figure 2

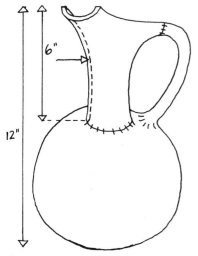

6"

12"

Figure 3

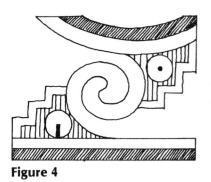

Figure 4

4. Trace your pattern onto the clay.

5. Form the neck and spout by rolling out a flat slab of clay about ¼ inch (.6 cm) thick and cutting it as in Figure 2.

6. The height of the neckpiece should equal that of the bottom of the coiled pot. Measure the pieces so they are in proportion to each other. The total height of the pitcher with the neck should be about 12 inches (30 cm).

7. Smooth the base of the neck onto the jug opening. Curve the spout slightly outward.

8. Roll a coil to make the handle.

9. Fit the handle between the neck and the base of the jug. Smooth the ends of the handle into the form.

10. Check all places where you have joined pieces of clay together to be sure that they are smooth and well fastened.

11. Let the clay dry.

12. If your school has a ceramic kiln, ask your art teacher about glazing and firing your clay pitcher.

13. After your jug is dry, paint decorative motifs on it (Figure 4). If your jug is not made of fired clay, it will not be waterproof and cannot be used to hold cocoa. But it makes an attractive holder for dried flowers or leaves.

Eagle Knight Helmet

Magnificent plumed headdresses were worn by various individuals in Aztec society. The design depended upon the wearer's rank. Great chiefs wore ornate headdresses decorated with brilliant feathers. These were supported on huge wooden frameworks on their backs. War helmets were more decorative than functional. Warriors were identified by the emblems on their helmets.

The noblest warrior classes were the Eagle Knights and the Jaguar Knights. Jaguar Knights wore jaguar skins into battle. The jaguar's open mouth formed an enclosing cap for the warrior's head. The knight appeared to look out from between the jaguar's jaws. Eagle Knights wore helmets shaped like an eagle's head. The helmets had huge beaks, bright eyes on each side of the head, and colorful arrays of feathers streaming out the back of the head. Sometimes the feathers covered the whole body. The long colorful feathers at the rear formed a tail. Other helmets, shaped like tigers, pumas, and snakes, were made of paper, cloth, bone, and feathers.

Materials you will need:
Poster paper or any other flexible cardboard in sheets 22 × 28 inches (55 × 70 cm); ruler; tape measure; pencil; scissors; stapler; crepe paper; rubber cement; masking tape; construction paper or other colored paper; feathers (optional)

1. Measure your head with a tape measure. Add about 1 inch (2.5 cm) to this for overlapping the ends of the headband. In our example, 21 inches (52.5 cm) + 1 inch (2.5 cm) = 22 inches (55 cm). If your headband measures only 22 inches (55 cm) including overlap, you can lay out each strip across the full width of the poster paper (Figure 1). If the headband is larger than 22 inches (55 cm), use the paper lengthwise. Cut out a strip that measures 22 inches (55 cm) (or your headband size) × 8½ inches (21.25 cm).

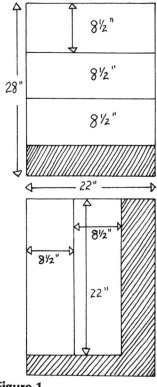

Figure 1

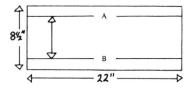

Figure 2

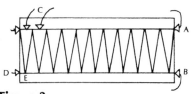

Figure 3

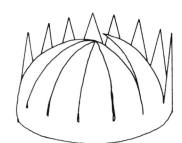

Figure 4a

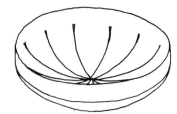

Figure 4b

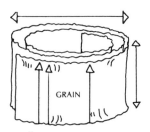

GRAIN

Figure 5a

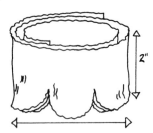

2"

Figure 5b

3. Set up one piece of poster paper as shown, with the long sides at the top and bottom. Measure, mark, and draw lines A and B, each 1½ inches (3.75 cm), inside the long edges to make the headbands (Figure 2).

4. Hold a ruler along line A. Mark point C 1 inch (2.5 cm) from the left edge. Then mark points every 2 inches (5 cm) from C to the end of the line. Hold the ruler along line B. Mark point D at the left edge, then mark point E 2 inches (5 cm) from C. Mark points every 2 inches (5 cm) from E to the end of the line.

5. Draw lines to connect the points (see Figure 3) to the end of the strip. Cut along the dotted line, but do not cut through the 1½ inch (3.75 cm) headband beyond lines A and B. Round off the points. This will make cutting much easier.

6. Connect the short ends of the piece, making a ring. Overlap the ends about 1 inch (2.5 cm). Hold the ends of the headband together and try it on to see if it fits around your head. Staple the ends twice to hold. Gather the five points together. Overlap the tips as shown (Figure 4a), and tape them. After taping, staple the tips together. Then gather the remaining five points, overlap their tips, and tape and staple them together. To join the halves, place helmet with the *points down* on table and press gently on headband until halves fit together and overlap slightly (Figure 4b).

7. To decorate the helmet, select the colors you wish to use. Cover the helmet with glued-on strips of crepe-paper fringe (see Figure 5a). To make fringe or feathers, cut across a roll of crepe paper to make strips 2 inches (5 cm) high and at least 24 inches (60 cm) long. Then refold the strips as shown so they are about 2 inches (5 cm) high and 3 inches (7.5 cm) wide when folded up. Cut scallops or points along one edge (Figure 5b). Cut several strips for each color you will use and cut more lengths as you need them.

8. Beginning at the bottom of the headband, brush on a line of rubber cement and press on a strip of fringe with the scallops pointing down (Figure 6). Allow this first row of scallops to hang over the bottom edge of headband. Add a second layer, overlapping the first about ½ inch (1.25 cm). Repeat, adding and overlapping layers until cardboard is covered (Figure 7). Cut out a crepe-paper oval about 2 inches (5 cm) long and glue it on the top of helmet to cover the edges of the last layer of scallops.

Figure 6

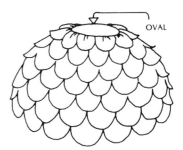

9. Make the beak, horns, crown, and other decorations from colored or plain cardboard covered with glued-on crepe paper. For example, cut the beak from a piece 4 inches (10 cm) by 5 inches (12.5 cm) (Figure 8). Leave a ¾ inch (1.87 cm) by 2 inch (5 cm) strip at the wide end of the beak. Cut this strip to make four tabs ½ inch (1.25 cm) each ¾ inch (1.87 cm) deep. Then fold the first tab to the right and the second tab to the left. Repeat this with the remaining two tabs. Glue or staple the tabs to the helmet (Figure 9). Tuck them under the crepe paper so they are not visible.

Figure 7

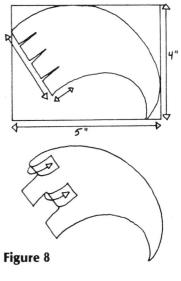

10. Cut the eyes from colored paper or foil and glue them on the helmet on each side of the beak. The eyes should be about 2 inches (5 cm) wide by 1½ inches (3.75 cm) high (Figure 10). To make the pupil, cut a small circle in a contrasting color and glue it onto the eye. Add eyelashes by making two strips of fringe and gluing them above the eyes. Make eyebrows out of construction paper and glue them above the eyes (Figure 11).

11. Cover up any areas where the materials do not join neatly by cutting small pieces of contrasting colors of crepe paper. Fasten them on as needed.

Figure 8

Figure 9

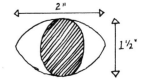

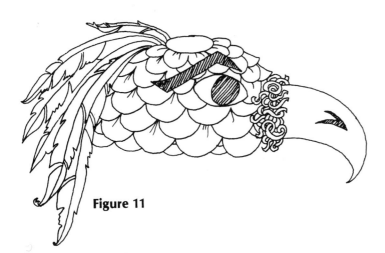

Figure 11

Figure 10

Index

Aztec hot cocoa, 15

Barter system, 5
Bas-reliefs, 21–23

Calendar, 8
Carved relief, 21–23
"Children of the sun," 11
Chocolate, 27
Clans, 4
Cloak, decorated, 18–20
Cocoa jug, 27–28
Cocoa recipe, 15
Codices, 6–7
Cortes, Hernando, 3
Crafts, 3–4

Day signs and numbers, 8–10
Diet, 14–15
Drum, 24–26

Eagle knight helmet, 29–31

Fire-baked sweet potato, 15
Foods from the New World, 14–15

Glyphs and codices, 6–7

Headdresses, 29
Helmet, eagle knight, 29–31
Hieroglyphics, 6
Huehuetl, 24
Huitzilopochtli, 11, 12
Human sacrifices, 5, 11

Jaguar knights, 29
Jug, 27–28

Life-style, 4

Mask, mosaic sun god, 11–13
Mexico City, 5
Montezuma, 5
Mosaic mask, 11–13
Music, 24

Nahuatl, 5, 16

Octli, 27

Religion, 5, 11

Salt dough recipe, 12
Society, 4
Sweet potato recipe, 15

Tenochtitlan, 3, 4, 6, 21
Teponaztli, 24
Tilmatli, 18
Tonatiuh, 11
Turquoise cloak, 18

Valley of Mexico, 3
Weaving, 19

Xiuhtilmatli, 18
Xocoatl, 27